CW00742746

Books by JL Williams include *Condition of Fire* (S
Marlin (Shearsman, 2014), *Our Real Red Selves*
House of the Tragic Poet (If A Leaf Falls Press, 2016).
dialogues through poetry across languages, perspectives and
form work, visual art, dance, opera and theatre.

Published widely in journals, her poetry has been translated into Dutch,
Spanish, Turkish, Polish, German, French and Greek, and she has read at poetry
festivals in Scotland, Turkey, Cyprus and Canada. Williams wrote the libretto for
the opera *Snow*, which premiered in London in 2017, was Writer-in-Residence
for the British Art Show 8 in Edinburgh with the artist Catherine Street and plays
in the poetry and music band Opul. www.jlwilliamspoetry.co.uk

"For some reason, slightly unfathomable, I am reminded of a forest we visited on
Japan's northern island of Hokkaido where the annual winter ice festival is held.
The forest is sprayed for days by the local fire department, but not before flowers
and colored lights have been hung within the branches, so when the whole forest
turns to crystalline ice, the lights burn from within, the whole crystal forest glows,
and when you walk there, flowers look out from the ice, arrested in full bloom. It
is all so unexpected, and so extravagantly beautiful—something essential in such
crystallization, and with fire in its core. Well, this vision returned to me reading
your manuscript."
—Eleanor Wilner

On *Locust and Marlin*

"It's the real thing I like it a lot! Internal variety... So many different kinds of
poems—'Learning to Love the Present' and 'Blinding' and 'Isn't the Start' and
the very last poem (such an emblem of poetry-in-general there) are by the same
author! I liked reading your earlier work but this... Just this."
—Stephen Burt

"This is a collection of grandiose, visionary poems about the nature of life and
death."
—Greg Thomas

"...the haunting, incantatory poetry of JL Williams."
—Chris Powici

Cover design by Anupa Gardner
www.anupagardner.com

JL Williams

After Economy

Shearsman Books

First published in the United Kingdom in 2017 by
Shearsman Books
50 Westons Hill Drive
Emersons Green
BRISTOL
BS16 7DF

Shearsman Books Ltd Registered Office
30–31 St. James Place, Mangotsfield, Bristol BS16 9JB
(this address not for correspondence)

www.shearsman.com

ISBN 978-1-84861-537-3

Cover art copyright © Anupa Gardner, 2017.
www.anupagardner.com

Contents

for RJ Iremonger

you on the horizon

After Economy

First they choose the forest with the most trees,
then they bind each tree in strings of brights.
Then they bring electricity to the roots,
covering the plugs so as not make fires.

Then they drive the firetrucks up,
it is winter, you remember—each red truck shiny as a new toy.
Then they unwind the hoses, embrace the soft tubes
and three people at each wheel begin to turn.

The first rinse takes some time, a glassy sheathing,
the second ices each branch quick and soon
the entire frozen forest glitters and shimmers
from within—each bulb encased in ice

a mouth through which the final word
of the world is shining out; *light, light.*

Antelope

In our hollow horns, music.
Beyond the long slope of stone,
shallow where myriad anemone bloom,
eels were raised for Antioch Caesar's blessing.
Bounce now, 'blouson of white like mist' he said,
where under water is blue and bellow below,
her hair a gold bubble shaft, his
white hands, beneath the water, like ivory
and art and I am. Bold, blow, he says
I am a boundary, and boundless.

Then when the great plains were covered
in snow as white as ivory,
we watched the last antelope,
like a dream of what man had been, bounding the drifts
and where his airy horns had broken off, music blew out
as if from French horns, women's mouths,
the caves we enter into.

Opacus

The wing of the plane
slicing through heavy mist.

Time slows down, or you become
part of geological time.

Somewhere rock
is turning into diamond.

Somewhere glass
of a very old greenhouse
is shattering.

Iskele Super Tamam

Some room three hundred years of light in it
No furniture a branch with six flames of magnolia
The body on the floor is half in darkness half in light
The skin of the body is half dark half light
The tongue of the body is speaking in all tongues
The walls are so white I polish them and polish
What floods my mind is a thousand years
Of river pushed to the tops of trees
And stones rubbing stones as stones rub skin
Into the shapes of this body this very body

&

He says in Arabic
he sings he sings he sings
He says in Arabic
in words of bird script
in words of sky script
these words are written by birds on the sky
He says in Arabic
it is the dark burning
The words I remember
are from another poem from another sky
where it is darkness
has power to heal
I realise also
that what he says
is also what I overheard some time
in some place it was some question
asked to the sky by birds
No one here is really from here
except for the trees
In Arabic the words
are weightless in Hungarian
the words are heavy jewels

&

There is sea there is land
There are vast tracts of undeveloped land running from hand-shaped
mountains to the sea
There are houses half-finished, human-sized dollhouses, living rooms
and bedrooms filled with air
The air smells of salt and soil and green leaves
Sometimes mimosa sometimes lemon flower sometimes bougainvillea
There are birds calling morning prayer and skinny cats and pregnant cats
and out of the dryer fluffy cats and a tiny wild dog barking a wolf

How do we love everyone how do we fight how do we fight complacency
how do we wake how do we wake up how do we play how do we play
fight how do we win how do we win kindness how do we play

we go to Othello's castle we go to the Venetian palace we go to the poet's
prison overlooking the garden once this mosque was a cathedral the tree
outside was born in 1299 it doesn't practise religion

I am not from my home or from my new home completely. In this third
culture I have no flag, I speak no language but my own. There are many
third cultures and in each our homes are our tents and our passports are
our tongues. I am not a colonist I am a traveller

&

You say to go away but I will not go away.
You ask me to be quiet and for an eternity
I am quiet. But as you say this poem
is a poem we are all writing, I recognise
your words in my poem my words in your poem,
his words in her chest her words in his sails
their words in their hearts those very old words
in this newborn poem, my love there is no sadness
breathing could not forgive my love without breath
I can't even stop loving you my love

this poem may die some evening
in a garden by the sea when dusk is blushing
up from the earth her eye of moon her hair of bats
but we won't be there
to witness the light stop shining

&

don't be afraid
just cuz
you can't stop love

New Aesthetic

the whale carcass on the beach with nearly all the flesh washed away
the taste of those salty bones defamiliarising words

Asterism

You cough out a mouthful of glitter and I see stars.

Did you forget your dream again? In the long pool, bodies and stars.

There is a threat coming from other people, but really it is because
    there is a star inside you sucking everything toward it.

On your forehead, a star, here, and a star, here.

Vastness is not darkness, it is the light within the star.

The light hits you and I see a tattoo with stars.

In all the broken places, constellations.

Once there was a universe with no people in it, just stars.

Disgusted with yourself, you close your eyes and implode.

Forgotten cellar in Egypt in which there is a 6,000-year-old map
    of distant stars.

Stone whose constellations shift in time with stars.

History, like the Rhine

As we said, history, like the Rhine, passes through a castellated region, and like that of the river, this stratum begins and ends suddenly.
Samuel Lucas, *Secularia; or, Surveys on the Mainstream of History*, 1862

()

The way you licked my leg
was how a man would lick.

I bought you. Thus I had every right
to free you.

My hand is broken because I built
every castle history lapped,
that damn river
whose silver veins
seam the skin of the world.

Between the turrets
I carefully cut
as a child with an automatic saw,
was the space in which
my whole life would take place.

It's not about dreams.
It's about the way I lick.

       Baby you forget
       this jazz quartet
       doesn't know
       how to end the song.

()

Ezra walked from castle to castle
in the footsteps of the ancient bards.

Later in the birdcage
in a Pisan piazza he cried
the words, the birds.

There is a poem translated from the Scottish
to Italian in which the bird species changed.

()

From the hoof of the fountain unicorn
in the courtyard of the palace in Linlithgow

       I stare at the wall
       as if my eyes
       are butterflies
       pinned to green baize.

JAMES ALIEURS (Ever in Bondage)
BELLE A VOUS SEULE (Beautiful to You Alone)

       That's what
       the bosses say,
       says the sign.

My hand a piece of silk
in the burn, your tongue
sliding up the inside of my leg, the fire
raging in a hearth big enough to cradle
twenty able-bodied men.

       Between my thighs
       that unspeakable crystal
       you dreamed
       in this life or the next.

The time of castles
was also my time
but this time
is also my time.

     James Alieurs
     Belle A Vous Seule
     The words
     flow over
     ma langue.

How to Mourn

All day long I stare at the flowers outside,
watch them grow up, walk around and fly.

Lie about your death, no one cares.
The smiles of the mourners you paid,

laying of the concrete stone, atonement
always more than you could afford.

I shimmy down the trellis, shatter jasmine scallops.
These fragrant snowstorms aren't for you.

Ban thoughts of failure now you're dead.
It is by running through heady night

with arms up and eyes closed
we learn the landscape of home.

Here I am, naked, panting on the powdery
earth of your grave.

Behave. It doesn't matter. We'll make love again.
We'll make love again.

Georgian Gallery

after Sequencer *by the artist Benedict Drew*

I feel the sound increasing all around me.
Then it breaks off, it's as if someone
is beating the giants who live
upstairs, on top of the mountain.

The scene is changing. All the time
it is as if the landscape
is changing.

I think we may be changing
the landscape.

It may be that there is a drone
there is a drone
I think I hear a drone.

This is how a drone sees,
yellow, trembling, in fast-forward, trembling,
melting, lava-like,
the land is changing.

Behind the landscape is a mountain. In front of the mountain
is a glowing sled.

I mean a glowing
harness.
I mean a glowing
rucksack frame.

I mean that before and behind
the mountain there is a landscape
which can be perceived

by the low-flying,
whose ears are attuned to

silence, only now the internal sounds of the body.

A pink portal, a vagina mouth, the opening
through which no sound
pours.

Two ears attached
to a body of tent poles.

'Speak into the ear'

that's what he said but
someone forgot to put on the headphones.

If only I could stand
and whisper these words
into the ear,
he would hear me
as if I was whispering
into his ear.

There was a time when
I was close enough
to hear colour, to see sound,
I remember that in the dream
there was a sailing ship,
I kept washing up on different beaches,
the taste of the sand was always
in my nose, the feeling of the salt
was always
in my ears, I mean
the sound of the salt,
I mean, the heart of the water
was my heart and I was a whale

or all of nature
was also
all of me.

The way rocks hear,
the way lichen whisper,
the way people millions of years ago
scratched their DNA code
into a cave wall deep underground,
the way a man walks past me, bearded,
all in black, carrying a bag, head raised,
full of sound.

All the body and all the organs of the body
and all the wetness below the crust
pulsating in time to the

stretched

drone

feather rock

fast forward lichen
rock pool
feather rock

fast forward
civilisation

time was
a city there then a forest
then a city then a forest then water
then a village then
ice then a city then water
a forest that grows in a circle
then changes to the shape of a liver

then changes to the shape of a heart
then changes to the shape of a diamond.

A woman in the centre of the forest
has dug a hole a mile deep.

Belly sounds,
blood sounds,
mouth sounds,
cell sounds,
marrow sounds.

When mosses grow they listen
to the blood in the rock flow.

'Who can live
on the blood of the rock?'

Only the lichen know.

Somewhere in the forest,
the woman has made a hole
two miles deep. She is digging,
the pink hole
is damp around the edges.

In the wooden building
at the base of the mountain
a man sits by an extinguished
fire. (o fire whose scent is the soul of wood)

There in the dark room
the scent of charred wood
and smoke circles
his bald head.

His eyes are closed
but he can see the woman
deep in the forest,
deep in the hole.

He can almost feel her wet lips
grazing the furred edge of his ear.

The man holds a chipped mug of whisky
in his hand, a hand hardened by wood.
His beard is rough moss,
his eyes are stones.

The woman says, 'my heart is a pink hole
into which you must come'.

The mug falls to the ground.

The wooden building
at the base of the mountain
is empty but for the scent
of the soul of the wood,
spilt whisky, sweat of a man.

Hey Did You Hear about the Kurds in Turkey?

Why so serious, Goldschmied? You forgotten how to laugh? What
kind of laughter, young man, did I ever have?
    —from the story *Resurrection* by Jakov Lind

Hey did you hear the earth is moving out of her orbit?

It's funny how people keep killing people,
it's a secret did you hear
the tiniest bugs even are less violent than inventive people.

It's the funniest joke, how this big old earth
is shifting up closer to Mars,
making the oceans splash around
and the earthquakes are working on population control.

No worries all the voices keep shouting—
that's what we're best at,
babble babble babbling babble babble,
did you hear the sound of the ocean
is the sound of all the bubbles jostling in the waves?
That's a little like laughing, all that impervious hot air.

A man and his dog with no money driving off a cliff in Ireland,
that's funny right? You laugh so much you cry,
or that old holocaust memory—you cry so much you laugh.

Either way, the ocean laughs up, takes off the clothes and fur,
leaves the salty bones on the beach for the beetles to find.

Beetles know how to build houses, they only talk in beetle language,
they don't laugh, they build their houses in the airy chambers of bones.

All those bodies in the street, don't forget there's a sniper
with his sights trained on your mother.
Don't expect her to pull your rotting body out of the road.
She'll join you anyway; die of shock, die of her hunger strike.

That's a joke I heard. There are lots of jokes like that.
I used to laugh all the time.

You ask me in your language why I'm not laughing?

You ask me why I do not laugh?

Woodnote

My home is the place where I dream I am not I someone
somewhere came to a quiet opening in the trees
having walked through the river they found sunlight
lost a soul is a punctuation mark for a sentence
that never ends when you come home feeling
you don't need to worry anyway between the trees
a woman is holding her hand in the gold light
heavy in the leaves of the silk trees the pressure
of dusk is condensing before it is dark I fall
and I am tired isn't there tenderness even then
in silence a floating garden between the trees
a deer with a face made of wild flowers its tail
a mountain river I broke the stem of a wild rose
and it did not scream its white blood dripped
over my fingers you'll remember a seed drifts off
all those lost plans of pine thrown on fires
each pail of water flying into a veined web each
droplet reflecting the death of the flame
in your eye forever forgotten the planets
are shifting an echo a shattered star a fist opening.

Water What Sounds

bells toll as in mist where
oil and flesh of seal mix plain song
held body come long before boats
before dream of sand by bottle god
green glass god eye green glass bottle god body
green glass dream of ocean ocean angels
mermaids narwhals bodies of elephant
skeletons of ivory long lost sea bed
mouthing clutch of anemone many-coloured
woman's hair woman's breath woman's tusk
cold bodies long sea green bottle skin
beyond bell-tone laughter of dumb buoys
in green bottle glass sea bone life plays
under water plain song long
this green eternal

Grief for the Lost Child

Imagine squeezing out
the moon through the throat of the universe.

When the channel of light through the mother's womb
becomes a channel of pain
the child cannot help but scream.

Each night the moon's
white light.

Who can deny that light
falls on exposed skin.

It wasn't that they wanted to hurt.
It wasn't that they wanted to suffer, or cause suffering.
They had been taught to suffer and thus cause suffering.

When the glasses and plates
broke amid screams
the child pressed the cat tighter.

The daughter in the attic
exhaling a lustrous cloud.

The daughter in the dark yard
trembling.

The pressure behind closed eyes.
The constantly sloppy house.
The broken door and spitting.
The inability to trust.
The toys sold to neighbours.
The fighting with no punishment.
The turning of sisters to enemies.
The mother raped and silenced.
The anger at the mother
who cannot stop the madness.
The doubt that one can be loved.
The disgust at one's own actions.
The longing to escape.
The imperative to forget.
The loss that accompanies forgetting.
The ache for what has been lost.
The desperate attempt to remember
something good.

As the little girl walked through the snow
she was accompanied by white light.
She came to the frozen river,
drank from a crack in the ice.
She changed into a white deer,
her eyes as blue
as the heart of the blue glass blue bird.

Light through clouds, through coloured glass.

Light through closed eyelids
red as rubies.

Light of a thousand stars.

Light reflecting in the lake.

Light of the headlights on concrete.

Light of the moon, white light.

The Immaculate Contraption

The storm that impregnated you last night was me.
Don't always say what I mean, it comes from my Catholic upbringing.
Mother used to make us pray and it took me longest to see
my brother's head rolling off into the distance, singing.

Up in the sky the speed at which I move is penetrating.
Birds wind up in my bowels, I shit out feathers at regular intervals.
No one will blame you for the little bastard you and I are creating.
I won't tell them she's the saviour of this god-damned fucked up world.

Think of me like a machine, some contraption with mile-long wings
far out over the sea with planets above and oil below,
my heart so filled with delight that the edges of my body are trembling,
like that first time you tasted pizza, 21 on the King's Road.

You're not special because I chose you, you're special because you're human.
Nothing you do ever again in this body will be forgotten.

Bread Song

!when you said! hell!
!did you mean! truth!
!or perhaps! heart! you said!
!red! red! red!
!in bed i! suffered!
!the mind ate! itself!
!the cat searched! the wall!
!each hole was! a bug!
!the pipes had! mice!
!the bread fell! to bits!
!when you said! hell!
!did you mean! heart!
!or maybe! truth!
!the sky turned! green!
!the hail fell! loud! you said!
!red! red! red!
!my head ate! the bread!
!the oven ate! the dough!
!the dough ate! the flour!
!the flour ate! the milk!
!the milk ate! the egg!
!the egg ate! the sugar!
!the sugar ate! the salt!
!the salt stung! the wound!
!red! red! red!
!I'm dead! you said!
!did you mean! hell!
!or possibly! truth!

una selva oscura

dear my light!
        (lover-light)
glow so

i can find you
in the forest i've
come to—darling—
        (lantern)
        (candle)
        (torch-flame)
survive me!
        (starlight)

all my leaves
a-tremble all my wings
fluttering all my eyes
wide open!

Little Mice

in the oven little mice
        scamper
THEY ARE YOUR PARENTS
telling the story of your birth
to every bread that bakes
        and the plumbers fill
        their mouths
        with that ASH BREAD
this doesn't make you a mouse
        because you have suffered
        as all angels suffer
the smell of the oven
will be wiped from your memory
and you will forgive
the people who built the oven
you will paint a portrait
of your parents in their youth
with legs and arms and eyes
        unburnt

The breeze blows honey-sweet perfume over us as we lie on the grass next to the honeysuckle bush. Later my head will split with migraine but for now this paradise holds no memory of winter but for a few dead leaves. You say that each year thankfully brings you closer to the end and that's what makes intellectual joy possible—the pleasure of knowing it is finite, for you at least, the suffering is finite.

> Yellow bell-shaped bud,
> death is in you as is life,
> and this pure perfume.

Selenotropism

I bore very slowly
my head toward the moon's light,
because my white petals
desired some touch beyond word.

Only in the white light
could my wings open, and my face—
innocent, as it was then, near birth—
welcomed death with no fear.

Or fear was natural in me, as was
the stomping of hooves over thick ice
and heavy snow, while deep in the white-blue
coldest of cold waters

whales swam in moonlit
circles and sang their low-pitched,
high-pitched harp song.
My body left behind

no longer troubled me.
Do not cry for the day I never saw,
the flight through oak leaves
was nothing compared to

lifting toward your white face.

Basin

mother in the clematis gathering white washing
gold horse throws its mane
gold hairs on her legs
rise eyes trace the horizon's
emptiness filled with sweet eggs
whipped to meringue almonds
polish of beeswax in leather
cotton dripping in white sun

GLASSY SUDS MOUTH BUBBLES

your hand brings the wax flower
in the bell—the bee—calls your name
you open your mouth surprised

bee enters your throat comes alive

GOLD TONGUE GLEAMING HONEY

deep in your centre a wax ball

MELTS ALL SILENCED BY HONEY

bee makes of you a white flower
mother calls from the horse's back

YOU ARE RINGING RINGING RINGING

bright as a bronze bell
peals you sing

life is the opening
through which we taste

Market at Golgotha

In the garden the stems of flowers
are the spears of the legionnaires
who aimed between the ribs of Jesus.

Women collect the tears
of the soldiers in crystal vials,
sell them to make enough money
to buy out their pimps.

Except for one whore, my mother,
who prefers the truth.

arroyo where last you

who in sleep dreams
and weeps for dreams
dead horses inability
move toward the desired
thirst wake both wet and dry
taste of sand cactus water
hot tanned legs feel
brown hair soft as muzzle of a woke horse

flail in the heat a vulture bent from sky

good enough for him
good enough for
beyond the good
bad beyond
that love

hairs and thread
thick rubbery
thin flexible
endless playing out
strands of hot glass
rope sewn
devils split cheek elastic thread
offering

this lit theatre
tying
broken things
cornbread and black coffee
chestnut smoke
sweat stained saddle leather

forget to wake you
duty to wake
wake you treachery gunshots
wake you panting
wake you

still sleeping
white flesh beneath my collar

boys lit the fire
ate supper coyotes
sang pine trees
the wind
how dark winter when the sun goes

slept in a circle heads
on saddles horses
learned to keep close
our language
their breaths
the long lost ocean

does not understand
the words hazy skein of dusk
in my mouth her man
has a boys hands
soft unable to shuck

vulgar gold
dont stop a man
dying

slept not far from a creek
last night couldn't hear a heart beat
for the water you
forgot beneath the noise
your aspirations the cobalt
of his eyes the racing water

Almost

I want to hold you under water until you stop struggling
then raise you again, watch you remember how good it is to breathe.

Wealthy children embellish their skins with cuts and burns,
starve in waxy houses to change into matchsticks.

I want to pour wine down your gullet holding your nose,
explain I come from a womb laced with wire and light.

Cars drive off bridges, buildings are downed by small planes.
Mothers in kitchens have no tools to cut the raw meat.
The meat is poisoned and greenish, it smells of a flood.

I want to cover your mouth and eyes with my hands,
release my grip when your tears lubricate tense palms.

Nostalgic technophobes cower beneath a gas globe.
Circumference of its orange cast grows more narrow.
Men and boys shove women toward its iron post.
They tell each other how good it was in the old days,
pointing out beautiful clichés like powder, mellifluence.
Armies of nano-economies dilute the city,
buoy me up as ants erecting an altar.

I want to watch you crush your scion in hopelessness,
beg you to stop, explain that you're almost ready
to appreciate your particular, exceptional gifts.

House of Rivers

Running, always running
as if to escape

the bronze eagle's raised
fist of claw,

the trout's belly blushing
at death's approach.

He bottles each river
at the river's mouth,
binds in glass the gurgling
urge to run.

I wake
straining like water.

Crèche

Summer brightly retires holding her gowns and fruits close for warmth
breaking   breaking
eggs   sun each morning over the sill
in the grocery store
a sharp pain   again   tho I thought it closed   this wound.

In a country where letters
cannot be delivered
let me write you one
that must never be delivered.

When there is no you and all the buildings
open their doors unto precious virgin palisades.

Did I imagine as a child this demon loneliness
or was he always my compatriot?

Peter whose wolf I will spend my best days hunting
and who may devour me for all I know
which is not yet enough.

'Look, there… untouched millions.'
(Can you remember how the marvellous butterflies sleep?)

I Love You and Your Rainbow Machine

My husband levitates at night
   —from the poem *Archipelago* by Jane McKie

()

When I pull my pants down
and see the blood
I know it is your white head
beating the drum.

All the staff at Harrods marching,
pens in your pocket,
a thousand widows glancing at once as I
kneel on the grand dais,
knife in hand,
aching for quiet,
your rainbow machine on my tongue.

All I need
is to open my mouth
and rise.

()

It isn't what birds do.

When it first happened
the priest was saying,
'all his holes'.

The light through the glass
was rainbow, all
was rainbow—I
was light and, floating
over the altar the congregation
gasped as the priest sang
'Holy, Holy, Holy
Mary, Mother of God'.

()

You take me to the attic
to show me your rainbow machine.

You pull the string and the hatch opens,
the ladder folds down.

Creaking, each wooden step
takes the weight of each foot.

Your feet in your socks.

We have to bend, the ceiling is low
and insulated.

Boxes of old ornaments
glint in the light of the torch.

I think you might kiss me, but instead
you open a silver box.

Light in a silver box.

All then is colour, someone shouting
from far below…

'Holy, holy, holy!
Mary, mother of God!'

()

O Savannah,
O Helium,
O Wretched Epiphany…

By the time I lay the knife down
every person in the room
remembers the brilliance of the womb.

()

What I wanted to say was
that when I woke up
I turned over
and your side of the bed was cold.

Blood was spilling down my leg.

The attic hatch was closed.

Outside the dawn
pressed her face against the window
and I swear
holy holy holy mary mother of god
a rainbow
lifted me up.

Watching *Breaking Bad* you realise both that your evil stepfather, similarly, sacrificed himself to his own personal disappointments and that Walter White is the character in the old story who forgets to ask the genie for the ship in which to bring the treasure home before he loses the magic lantern. While it might seem as if he has not achieved the full extent of his dream, the more concerning assumption is that he has, and that his true desire has always been to destroy his family and free himself from his suburban nightmare. Even if that means the rest of his life alone on a beach with nothing to eat but rubies.

> The red glittering
> destruction of the self which
> is also the heart.

Desiderata Nocturne

The night a black glass prism.
The night a baguette of gold.
The night unstrung from the underskirt.
The night of the last exhale.
The crystalline quiver of stars.

The breath of the dragging possum.
The unsettling wish for mercy.
The car many miles off, away, uncertain,
front tires coated in blood.
The brush of wings on earth.

The park by the side of the road.
The smell of blood in the dark.
The slow heave of the gorge.
The glistering fire in the sky.
The distant vanity of cities.

The hand wiping the mouth.
The radio singing, 'My love,
return to,' a torrent of sudden
wind, the speeding bolt of truck,
the huff and then the dark.

Dark, this desire for space.
The wasteland stained star-white.
A lake speared with dead trees
whose white trunks stab the sky.
The ribs of angels up.

The pillow, the cabochon, the gleam.
The fall slow as exile.
The air exhaling by.

The grit of sand on skin.
The hit and hit again.

The night whose mouth is wide.
The sleep that hands make ready.
The sin and then the sacrifice.
The forgiveness of the light
whose burning kiss is time.

Blood on the Trees

"a car" "awash with blood" —Alice Notley

For a glittering ruby eternity
he stands in the road listening
while the stars burn crimson and the windows
shatter up the street
filling the air with
flashing red splinters minnows of blood
travelling at great speed

looking still
spray of blood down his cheek
memory of sunlight pane-ing crystal crosswise beam
chip in his grandmother's
bottle of perfume

falling from high above a missile
dropped like a leaf from a tree turning
a waltz in three *me me me*
with no regard for the scene children
playing in the yard father on a porch
swing of the old Mercedes' door
slow motion metal wing

what he takes in in a moment dazzles him
the great beauty and balance of everything
the marvel of a woman's lips the implausible
joy of being the papery bark of a birch tree
he wrote on as a child forming letters
by digging with his fingernails feeling the pulp
slide between the nail and the skin

when nothing is left of silence there is an echo
even if only birch trees can hear it
the blood on the trees is a testament the trees

are whispering names and numbers and places
and first loves and worst fears and sacred wishes
and secret plans and skeletons of poems
and passages of songs

'and the sun fell one last night fish
caught bronze mid-leap dusty ponies
neighing noses high crops
pressed toward sandy soil by the wind
the smell of burning smoky messages
no one left to interpret'

'how different it could have been caverns of ice
filled with light so much can be broken
with the merest tilting of a mirror
or stepping out over the alien crevasse
on a plank of glass he felt himself
become the heart of flying'

'deep in the sea
oysters with pearl eyes open
opal mouths for salt
crying for the blue fire
beyond Orion and
mercury anemone blooming'

a raven stands in the jade grass
still as a carving in onyx
watching the blood drip out of the car
soak into the soil dye the frond-like
curls of ferns

hold me no go quickly
talk to me slowly if at all
whisper so I can barely
touch me here touch me
for a glittering ruby eternity.

Europa

What was lost cannot be restored.—Aleksander Hemon

Living on this island lands me closer,
closer to the countless
dreaming tongues of the continent.

All you broke hand men, put your guns down.

The cider barrels filled with dead sparrows.

The warships have run aground, your father
and his father, they bones they bones.

Here graveyard, here bones—
black dog fucking young girl
England now *we heart you.*

Millstone metal in the factory
rusted in the heart of screaming
British White and the dead cod flopping
on the poisoned shore I told you this is not
the fault of bloody immigrants.

You think your babies are going to grow
with Mother Tongue in their mouths?
No my children, you hear that sound?
That sound?
They're choking on a balled-up Union Jack.

Between the red brick buildings,
between Queen Street and Number 10,
two Polish women are dancing.

They are singing English
with a Polish accent.

No, with an English accent.

They were born in England
and remember how their grandmothers
danced in the gas chamber.

They do this dance now,
they sing the old song,
they teach me to British dream.

By remembering I fold myself into you

No silence no present moment exists
in which you do not exist.

The men I adore holed up dreaming
eagles whose nests are bent into mist.

I was always waiting
for you my brother
lost on the road under the tree
whose pain is gold golden.
My father who I do not know.
My country who I do not know.

You are here finally
in the mouth of the bird
whose tongue is one I recognise,
whose tongue is the crab living in the mouth
replacing the tongue
saying all your food is mine finally
my love.

Poor bird without trees
whose home was given to the war,
who remembers the two-penny hangovers of men.

My only, my bird whose wing is pulling
via shoulder muscle tight within the belly
up up past the present,
past the observation of burning light
in clouds over sea to the boys on the side,
their privilege their impatient deaths their unwritten down.

Their wooden rifles carried into war.

Their horse-drawn carriage.
Their quiet mule.
Their mother's slip.
Their warm hay bale.
Their accumulation of birdsong.

In the Garden

The flowers are words.

See the bright blooms
coming out of green mouths;
begonias, peonies,
bell-like rhododendron.

Each sighing *breathe, breathe*
in the language of flowers.

Canto

When the ice on the pond moans,
a lover caught between
wanting you to get on with it
and wanting you to slide over
every inch
and the wind is yelping in the trees
and it reminds you of your dead cat
whose ashes are still to be buried,
whose weight you can still feel
as his life went away in your hand,
when the cold takes your mouth
and smacks it as if it was Russia
and the princess caught you in flagrante,
your ermine pants 'round your ankles,
your tarnished crown on the bed,
when the swords of light from the stars
push into your eyes
and the water pours from them washing
winter all over your cheeks,
when the gods beyond the castle
are cataclysms of light,
when the pillars inside you crack
and the sorrow freezes your marrow
then I will see you,
an apple,
a witness to hunger
and I will release you from your existence.

I will carry you through the broken gate and into the world,
a shiny, red, wet
crystal of possibility.

The Banished

looking in from outside where the fire is burning
looking in from outside so our hair seems to be on fire
looking into the empty house whose only
people are the forgotten memories of ourselves

looking in at the tides of dust and the peeling of mirrors
the peeling whose iridescence is reminiscent of shells
the pealing of bells signalling a memory about to appear
long-buried because of its too great pleasure

silent as the witches whose innocence welds the tongue
outside where we belong with the fire and the sea's glass
its waves of green astonishment lavishing the sand
the creatures of the deep and the wild salt

looking in at our own reflection with sleep-heavy eyes
as if a spell has been cast from which we cannot wake
our hands forever wet with the birth milk of the milkweed
our breath   our image in the painting   fading

The Disappeared

we have not known or met ourselves previously
pale fire blooms in our mouths the gold father

dies each night is born each morning
we enact love in air we do not copulate

the horns of planes impale us
we wrap ourselves around you

finger the pulse in your thighs
your heartful of tears

we wait with those of no homes as they die
nakedness does not embarrass us

we do not feed are carried along on the wind
we smell of seedlings and ferns

we sound like bells
as children comb their hair we learn to make music

we cannot see ourselves
we lose in mist

Infinity Song

wasn't it funny how nothing ever seemed to work
      jerking of slate and copper
there would be light at the end of the suitcase
      race to the starting line
a small package of breath
      death never comes to those who undress

the soul doesn't always fully emerge
      splurge on a cottage at the end of a dirt road
we stink of light the lighthouses flash
      splash glitter on the sea's eyelids
borne on waves of nostalgia so few of us
      blush anymore the dark prevents it
forward the white bird not the black bird
      furred gut of the dishonest mariner

I'd hoped to undress with the monarch
      stark piety of acolytes
butterfly the orange powder of his wings
      swings low sweet apostolic beatitude
doing too many things at once means
      screens bleat back the tick of the clock
the heart only has so many beats
      retreats an old house collapsing in on itself
each moment a candle in a windy night
      righteous thief who steals belief

helicopters descend and the woman's headdress
      caresses, unravels old man's skin
tremble with nothing to do but sleep
      creep between the shutters of the mind
powder in fluorescent tubes prevents breaking
      shaking light from trees whose branches are glass

passers-by on a cold night whose heavens
          leaven fear of restraint
milk across a woman's tongue
          strung pearls unstrung
onlookers in thrall spellbound weeping
          deeper than their reflection in the sea

the hole that could not close
          rose as if it were the moon
the wound that could not close
          chose to comment on the scene
bitter almonds and a hot wind rising from the east
          ceased to scatter rose petals on the palace floor
ghosts sleeping with the living tissue fingers
          stringers of insensible rhythms
interwoven with fingers of flesh

          meshed as lover's fingers mesh
golden eyes tipping back and forth between this world
          unfurled for all the sleepers to see
and the next (we are what ghost's dream)

          seem to see

death is not a doorstop time gives
          lives hews seethes scores frees
when you let go of it funny how when
          then never again
you really listen to the note the note
          choked stroked
becomes the only note you need
          bleed don't bleed
when you stop looking you are lost
          frost on tendrils
the bird wings suddenly seem like hands
          strands
all the animals kneel

Transhuman

Echoing static on screens.

How do I feel, now; with electricity.
How do I speak, now;
of the cacophony of light.

A gull calls, and no one hears it
though it is recorded for posterity.

I Enquire of You

In order to laugh in darkness at the sound,
to transcribe the inexplicable.

In order to connect with the eye as with a bridge,
to make of the body a sounding board,
to understand as a plaice does
water with its gills,
as a dipper does air with its feathers,
as a man does skin with his tongue.

In order to exist, to reproduce
the utter enigma of industry,
to conjure the porcelain of moonlight,
to say 'light through cranberry glass',
to sleep in a hammock and wake in light
drenched with the wetness of dreaming.

In order to know all the words for blue,
to find a new way to describe all power
via the names for blue:
uliuli blua mawaawa
zils blau glas
manga azurine obwato
ixki azul sinine luhlaza bleu.

In order to know that words are born of places
they are first said and that poems of death
come from the land where the sun never shines,
poems of friendship come from the land where the sun always shines,
poems of silence come from the land where the snow always falls,
poems of pain come from the ocean where the only water
must be sucked from the slave's torn out heart.

In order to understand that on an island
bodies of birds were used for candles,
bird beaks opened and wick threaded down
the bird's dry throat and lit.

In order to know that the poet loved the bird,
that poems were written by the light of the bird,
that the poet knew the practise of preserving the bird,
of flattening the corpse and folding it like a book.

In order to smell the smoke in the dark room,
to know what the words mean though you don't know the words,
to recognise the name being spoken by the wind.

Belief

It breaks so slowly
it is almost like coming together.

My friend, who is both a philosopher and a psychoanalyst, sends me a video in which he explains Žižek's interpretation of the male unconscious desire to see the woman he is married to as a man; her red dress and high heels render her more manly in the part of his unconscious which leads to his erection, as he interprets her dress and heels as a costume hiding the real male underneath the skirt, making the fantasy of her as a man even more powerful. This helps me to understand the fear my ex-husband had for the 22-year-old woman I was when he married me—both a suitable foil for his unbearable fantasy and a naive seductress with boyish, cropped hair.

> Your hand on the back
> of my neck, all my questions
> buried in your mouth.

'There's No Such Thing as a Long Walk Down a Short Plank, Is There?'

She said. 'Fuck it all. Unhinged? Exhausted?
Want a solution? Drink up. Snort up.'
I laughed. Bob laughed. Susan
choked on her tequila. 'You're so painterly,
with your broke bottle sticking out of your pocket,
your boys round the corner waiting with the dog.'
'Drink up,' you say, bleeding, thinking
I can't smell it. 'Breath like sugar.'

She said. 'You might as well hold your arse
or you'll drown.' I couldn't believe
any clown could be so crass. The stars are in the pool.
The girl is in the pool unrolled like a piece of aluminium
foil. Her eyes are blue. Her skin is blue. Her hair is blue.
The water is purple, gleaming. 'Splurge.'

She said. 'It's payment, currency. That's what breath is.'
Let's burn out together, be stars falling
from our cradle in the sky. What else before we die?
Bleed, blue blood, electric neon buzzing silence
and the toaster at the bottom of the pool,
its cord the tail of some ancient beast so many millennia old
it's made of rubber or salt. 'The fried up hearts of stars.'

She said. The opal in the castle is under
the slab of the king's right thigh.
Die? When the chaos is in my mouth and the cameras
are finally blind and the money's drifting off
into screams and atmosphere?
I'd rather find some quiet by the river,
some bread made of water and oats,
some old woman who's survived long enough
to teach me how to dance. 'Now *that's* romance.'

Paradigm

As if it were a star lifted up and out of the eye,
the truth sparks in the mirror, on the table.
It's a chip of a diamond, a snowflake on a navy sleeve,
a pale seed, a miniature key.
All this can be exactly as you wish it to be,
it winks. As the slow bend of the spoon suggests,
the shift takes place not in the metal
but in the metal inside, that hot core
whose founder resides at the base
of the peak of your being.
What molten pour will bleed
a bright river
this time? Time, whose face itself
is ours.

The Home of Hunger

A lion's head, mouth hanging.
The statue's hand outstretched.

Footsteps on the river.

Success in spite of so many odds,
frozen conquest.

The eagle cries. The whole world
is a weight.

> *flute that nearly fractures*
> *ice shining so bright it nearly*
> *blinds*

What we cannot have
is burning from the inside out, fire whose secret
must never be revealed.

Good Work

Walk to the river
like light on the river whose heart
cannot drown,
is never thirsty even in the desert—no compass
or pouch filled with water.

Do you hear the bombs in the valley?
They are quiet,
muffled as footsteps on salt.

In the desert of salt the sea is a body
cured in snow.
It crunches, breathes slowly.
Footsteps in snow.

We die in a river of salt,
light on water,
bodies white angels sunk without hate or remorse.

We die melting in one another's
river of salt,
water on lips
thirsty as the borderless desert.

Do you hear the soldiers' song?
It is quiet as a compass
in the desert of lead.

The water,
hot to the touch,
undrinkable but for the dead.

We die in the desert blackened by sun,
whitened by salt.

We die of thirst in the desert,
saltwater lapping at feet
seared by the bombs, the sand, the salt.

We die staring into the sun,
eyes whitened,
wings on our cheeks.

The sun is a river of salt,
a white scarf blowing in the desert.

Bombs fill the sky with clouds.

Can you hear the language spoken by the clouds,
by the salt-crusted lips of the desert?

The words are quiet,
heart-broken,
afraid for you.

They say, 'You are water, salt, desert,
her eyes opening again
when she was lost forever,
opening again,
white salt crumbling like sand.'

They say, 'We die
in the mirrored rooms of our dreams,
wake each morning in one another's arms
thirsty as salt,
thirsty as desert,
thirsty as light for the river.'

It is a couple of days after the referendum and this postcard comes through the mail slot. It says 'leave motherfucker leave fucking immigrant'. Then another one comes though, and another. Soon I can't get my door open because of all the hate mail. I try for a window and some arsehole with a 'we won now get the fuck out' t-shirt is jumping up and down and shouting. Same with the back door, and there's a crowd of them. I go to the sofa with a Stella in one hand and a knife in the other.

What I see in the
surface of the knife is the
face of a true Brit.

Letters from Home

Keep me with you anyway,
the masses frighten me.
My identity is hard-won. I don't like orgies.

The grass-faced woman, her '30s hair, her khaki pants.
The gramophone looks like an animal in her hands.
Marty, what's a girl without a gun?

Raised children, corn, whatever needs growing
and already
dun with sun, sex-tendered.

Believe in, ripe, what? You said clearly
'No such thing as good
without a moral definition of good,'

but ice cream makes the kid smile anyway.
Say *thigh*. Say
her thigh sweet as vetiver.

Birds know, bird catchers too, another name for corpses.
Belinda winds the gramophone. Wooden doors open.
Flame-cast shadows flicker in mortal embrace.

You Are the Ear

The green sheath of the corn falls away.
The child's wounds close.

A woman stops crying. A man stops kicking a dog.
Someone turns from an invitation to betrayal.

Each kernel is gold, has always been
swollen with milk.

No one prays. The prayer is already
here as seed, as light.

Ithakas

It is cold and my horse has left me.
My armour is no longer shining.

Thin branch, scratches on skin.
Damp white butterflies lift.

Remember, beacon, our nights.
Only your flame keeps me stumbling through the birch wood.

Through Darkness We Realise Shining

on the eclipse of the sun in the year 2015, for Alexander Hutchison

The people in the old film called to me.
In the silvery light their hands and lips said
Behold, you will join us in death.

I have never been so afraid.

The people I passed on the streets were ghosts,
the pity I felt for the whippets and pigeons
shattered the lantern inside me.

In this strange new darkness, the lizard's tongue
flicked as slowly as an angel's.

My religious beliefs fell like ash in the hearth,
the last hot red coal turned grey.

I stood on the bank of the murky river,
smelling, to my horror, nothing. No rotting leaves,
no loose blood, no salt of a hundred fishes.

What appeared in the form of love
could hardly penetrate the darkness.

You joined me on the bank of the river
and scent returned with light; the sweet new grass,
the apple blossom, straw burning in the field.

Through drifting smoke I saw your face,
sun in each tear on your cheek.

Every time the darkness returns,
may we realise this shining.

Euskal Herria

...and they call me Anastasia [resurrection].
And they call her Gizane [Christ's incarnation]
from the Basque country.

There is beach enough for picnicking.
We eat air bread. We drink
air wine out of giant shells.

Gizane says *akelarre*.
Beyond the beach, darkness despite the sun.

Gizane is gone for the harvest.
Men heave. Onto the sand, *balea*.
I weep for her then eat her fatty flesh.

Gizane returns, old and pale.
Behind her the shadow, Basajaun.

Her eyes have gone wholly white.
She pulls back her lips.
I see the red drops on her gums.

Basajaun cackles and wheezes.

He raises a gnarled hand, shifts it about.
Gizane does a small dance.

The Germans raise their hands and Picasso gasps.
He has seen the first of the bodies shorn of skin.

The tree of Guernica shakes its needles
at the green sky screaming in the speech of trees
that only birds understand.

We build a city where once there was a city.
Sorgin trail from door to door
offering the wares of their craft. They sing

sorgin-haize, sorgin oilo, sorginorratz.

From their mouths appears what they intone.

Yesterday for your parlour I purchased a whirlwind.
You tell me it prefers the shady corners of the room
and makes a sound like breath in a coat of fur.

One Half is Night

Some days it is harder
to fathom the loss of light
and words come as peacocks do to water.

Nothing restrains night but day,
nothing holds against obliqueness but this clear heart;
a burst bulb working its love like a strung-out whore.

Callimachus, counter of volumes—
your patience reminds the legions that hope matters,
precision,

the strength to mark one's own
clock as it is stopping.
Graffiti paints over the prophecy,

the sun's red smear of lips
gives up a sprayed-on glimpse of last night's promise:
'I'll remember, I'll remember each lit thing.'

Will You Do That?

Is it sad, how all these wounds fall open, eyes?
Dynamic as chandeliers when the earth is turning.
Do fish have knees? Particular, resolute—you cadenza:
Lord, my country is a home with no name.
To translate there are words used, they are
not allowed now. Instead mouth:
'With the heat on it is difficult to breathe.'
Do you understand? Where I come from
the snow has a face. An old woman
stealing apples from a hotel lobby.

Dynamic as chandeliers when the earth is turning,
a pink veil swells around the lip of this horizon.
Corona, skull dish, an iced bun served in cream.
The bus thunders overland, glass in thousands of frames.
Beneath us, salty rivers pound fish.
Brass heads roll on a gallery sill.
Brass lizards cling to walls.
The graveyard holds the bones of dead Swedes.
Streets are low-lit, quiet and even
when the bells of the church toll it is politely.

Corona, skull dish, an iced bun served in cream.
A muslin dress floating on a black ground.
The lighthouse flash casts objects in negative frieze;
halo of light in the hall of a marble arcade, the space
created by pillars raising a ceiling.
What clean streets. What nice, unsmiling people.
Keep thinking of how to say
forbidden words, keep realising how to show
his flesh wetting the cartilage
in the knee of the fish where the infinite pulse is strongest.

Halo of light in the hall of a marble arcade, the space
caged by wolves is a pantomime of carrion.
French gangs ape whores' ecumenical song while
reindeer drop their furred eyelids in shame.
The familiar smell of burning tallow and cotton.
Grackles swarm a pagoda that hosts
jasmine tea, Mondrian squares, a girl who pulls a foetus from her nose.
Out over the ocean; aeoning lights.
Isn't it strange how a face looks through ice?
The end before the beginning, as in Christ's way.

Arcadia, Texas

The wheat is waving in the jukebox.

Young boys, your father's a pharmacologist,
a professional! Young cowboys,
he's built a manufacturing plant.

Get your shotguns ready!
Your engines revved up!

The police cows are wailing.
There is a god-fearing horizon,
and every body is on the stoop
of Daddy's kitchen saloon.

Mamma's dressed like a raven.
She's packed her valise with a flume.
It is suggested she exercise
at least three pints a day.
Religious desert, pour a blood carpet.
Madamoiselle has crystal breath at noon.

The president's in the belfry.
The smoke is in his eyes.
He's bombed again, like yesterday,
when both his feet when in his pants at once.

Succinct Madonna, how long have we been up?
Your hips are rounding with child.
Your breasts are bearing flag.
It would be immoral to burn you.

So stumble fields and dance!

This is our hay day, o great stretched middle of method loom.
Placate for the horn drifting through the morning.
It is the bull who kneels down first, sings hallelujah, dies.

While on the plane in a haze of cloud and reheated vegetable lasagna, it is difficult to remember what films I have watched recently and also what it was I had hoped to capture about that holiday when I was young—the wooden cottage on the shore of Lake Ontario that creaked in the night, the step-grandfather with his baroque sausages and gruff-sweet manner, the smell of salt and old wood, the field on the other side of the road where the grasses and flowers were taller than me, the dragonflies in every holographic colour bigger than my hand, the wet black cliff clambered down to the thrashing water, the unusual trip with my mother alone and the doll I wanted that she wanted to buy me that I wouldn't, couldn't, accept—the whiteness blanking out the entire rest of that summer, like these clouds.

> The single eye of
> the Cyclops impaled creates
> a life-sized cavern.

The Thousand-Petalled Night

nobody cries enough to mourn for us
my father when he was still in life
that reminds me now if my father

the mystery of my father

the mystery of the earth
opening all her mouths for us
opening her womb of fire
to embrace us

Bella
Leora
Inez
Isaiah
Jacob
Jonah
Nicodemus
Noah
Moses
Menelaus

the mystery of the earth
opening her soiled legs

Ezra
Indigo
Isaac
Ondine
Aria
Lana
Mabel
Maybelle

the mystery of the earth
throwing seeds to the wind

Jupiter
Juniper
Yarrow

mother
betrayal
religion

sister father love

if we talked about death more
maybe we would slow down
finally had some idea
between the translucent buildings
plastic, as in my dreams
pale pink, pale blue, pale yellow

if you dance with her
take pleasure

it doesn't mean
you have power
it doesn't mean you can have anything
it might mean
she has power

if spirits are memories anyway
of course there are ghosts

imperfect
worthy of love

I am no I
I am not *like* or *as*

her work is never finished
and her clock is never fixed she says
O yes, O yes
one day I'll find the time

the horses pulling the fire truck
the cardinals
the pomegranate beads
cupped in the palm of his hand

what was lost is lost
it's a new state of being
moss with jewelled beetles
fulgent black bottles
forest earth blood

white lamps or candle wicks
smudged black ends
brimstone and smoke
match lit and going out

dusty ink on your skin
portraits of saints
scenes of crucifixion

that night we climbed the mountain
stone stairs a thousand years old
only the moon to light
the cacti and their thorns
the silver globes of pomegranates
the silver globes of oranges
the tiny silver globes of olives on their branches
and the silver leaves of the olive trees
trembling in our wake
and then no moon
and only your voice
and our breath

and the heat of the stone
pulling us up
between the breasts of the mountain

the night we stood on the rooftop
and the air was liquid silver
and the silver dripped from our lips
onto the belly of the sea

when i walked through the mirror
and found you as a child
holding an acorn to the light
as if to see the life inside

when sound decays
it becomes
a new kind of sound

you on the horizon
floating on the water
a lotus flower rising from your head

four notes:
one from the west
one from the north
one from the east
one from the south

you are in the centre
i am in the centre of sound

it won't last long
but someday
someone will start to play again

sometimes i feel a breath, a hand
trailing its fingers in the silver water

Bounty

His wet skin, his five dark horses, his antelope horns, his long thighs,
    his lips.

There is a bruise above his breast beneath which beats the bronze drum
    of Tantalus.

Married to the daughter of a river god how
could he ever hold her, body rushing through fingers
himself neither one thing nor
always just out of

In Argos they stroke his bones, he whose soul is that of a man's,
whose body is that of a god's, resides where his mother made him
deep in the bowels of the earth where rubies and diamonds bloom.

Shaman, he fed his son to the earth and the earth
in her sorrow ate him and thus he must be buried and must
we all be buried, become like jewels, become bounty.

In the gold light some
cocooned secret is reborn,
opens its frail wings.

Notes and Acknowledgements

The poem 'After Economy' was inspired by generous words of the poet Eleanor Wilner, to whom I am most grateful for reading and responding to these poems in manuscript.

Many thanks to James Iremonger, Colin Waters and Bhikkhu Abhinando for their generosity in reading and responding to the manuscript.

Thanks also to Anupa Gardner for the cover image on this book and for helping me to see into the belly of the whale.

'Antelope' and 'Bounty' were first published in *The Wolf*.

'Market at Golgotha', 'arroyo where last you' and 'Almost' were first published online as part of the Dangerous Women Project.

'There's No Such Thing as a Short Walk Down a Long Plank, Is There?' was first published in *Ecstatic Peace Poetry Journal*.

'Desiderata Nocturne' was first published in *Molly Bloom* 6.

'Opacus', previously titled 'Heart's Flight', was first published in *The Compass*.

'By remembering I fold myself into you' was first published in *Like Leaves in Autumn: Responses to the war poetry of Giuseppe Ungaretti*.

'The Banished' was first published in *Innu Poetry*, a pamphlet produced for the Edinburgh International Book Festival 2015.

'Infinity Song' was inspired by rhythms in the poetry of Peter Manson.

'I Enquire of You' was written after learning that in 1786 Robert Burns had accepted a position as overseer on a Jamaican sugar estate. Had his first book of poetry not been such an immediate success, he would almost certainly have boarded ship and become part of the slave economy.

Ovid called Grozny 'The Home of Hunger'. Pliny the Elder's Natural History (AD 77-79) derives the name of the Caucasus from the Scythian *kroy-khasis* ('ice-shining, white with snow'). In Greek mythology the Caucasus, or Kaukasos, was one of the pillars supporting the world. After presenting man with the gift of fire, Prometheus was chained there by Zeus to have his liver eaten daily by an eagle as punishment for defying Zeus' wish of not giving the 'secret of fire' to humans. *Wikipedia*

'Good Work' was inspired by the film *Beau Travail (1999)* by French director Claire Denis.

'Through Darkness We Realise Shining' was commissioned by the 2015 StAnza International Poetry Festival as part of the University of Glasgow's *Bridging the Continental Divide* project for the translation of neo-Latin Scottish poetry.

'The Thousand-Petalled Night' was written for James Iremonger.

Lightning Source UK Ltd.
Milton Keynes UK
UKOW03f0316090317
296165UK00002B/188/P

9 781848 615373